Don't Miss Your Flight (Prevent Your Future Damage)

By

Bernard Benson Sarfo

Dedication

I dedicate this book to everyone in the world today.

"When wisdom entered into your heart, and knowledge is pleasant unto your soul, discretion shall preserve you, understanding shall keep you" (Proverbs 2:10, 11).

Introduction

Many of us make mistakes which cannot be healed by any balm or a word of comfort.

Others take things for granted without considering the outcome. This world has a lot of dangers that need consideration and the manner we live in.

Many are the things that cause us anxiety but many of us entertain it. There are so many things cause a wound that cannot be healed. We need to be careful in the way and manner we behave.

It is better to prevent them than to cure. It is better to look side and side before uttering your word.

This means we must be careful about our speech. It is late to say I am sorry, whiles it is against the law. The world is dying today because of regardless of the laws that govern nature.

Your joy can be my sorrow and your sorrow can be my joy because of our sinful nature. And that is not what it should be, but it is going on in our lives.

What must we know as human beings? Many are dying because of mistakes, and again many are wound because of wrongdoings.

My hurt can be your wealth and your wealth can be a sword to those who you shared with. The world we live in has a lot of misunderstanding and the incidents difficult to explain.

Whatever happened have a lesson and the notes we must take from it. Consider and think of whatever you are doing, not to hurt somebody's before and saying I am sorry.

Else you have done a foolish thing. Mind your word, mind your doings and be watchful.

It is too late to say you are sorry. This book is prompting us on the way we act deliberately to hurt others, and then cause ourselves damage. Then later say sorry through pretending.

Meanwhile, the unhealed mark has been caused to the brother or sister. Do away the wrong act and consider every word from your mouth.

In fact, there are many things in the world which God purposely created to test our faithfulness to him. And to help us to develop as human beings; and to maintain our perfect character that God has put in us.

It is not God purpose to put something that can cause our ruin. But He (God) put it there to help us keep on in good works in our lives.

In fact, every good thing is test by a negative to see how best that thing can last.

For example, when you made a car and then want to see how best it is, you must drive it on a rough road to see the condition about that car. Your todays deeds will predict the future result.

Contents Pages

1. What have you done?

There are a lot of happenings difficult to understand. This world has a lot of histories horrible to explain.

Many have failed in life and have brought bad results to themselves and their children.

One mistake can damage the blessing equivalent to the size of the sea water. Sin has cost us and has put our Lord Jesus Christ into death who exchanges his life for our life to death.

He has given us another chance to live again as without sin or stain. What have you done?

This question is asking you about your sin day and night. Have you stopped wrongdoing or planning to stop?

Many people are keeping on doing bad things. They purposely wrong like Cain of old.

Have you hurt someone to death some time ago by mistake? Or you still put people to death through your daily activities?

What have you done? All sin that man has committed have great magnitude. But the one who deliberately takes the life of someone will be replacing his or her life to that one whose life has been taken. God will request that souls from those murderers.

No human being canned creates his or her mate. Here, there is no way to put someone to death or taking his or her life, because of your needs. Human's life is precious and dear to God.

So, there is no way to cause someone's death. Those who engage in killings or taking other's life must take note that, God will request those souls to life or they will exchange theirs for those whose life has been taken. What have you done?

Never ever behave like Cain of old who murdered his brother because of envy. There are many activities causing other's life to death but many people are engaging in it.

Some people are engaging in killings their fellow beings. The world we live in has a lot of bad histories and the things difficult to comprehend.

Many people are engaging themselves only for money and food without thinking. But this world is not there only for moneymaking and food eating. It is our duty to know more about nature and God.

One thing everyone must think of or put in mind is to ask that; what will be my portion at the end?

There are many things done without thinking. What must we know as human beings? And what must we do as human beings?

This world is not there for fun, but it is for accountability. Every work must be accountable.

Every word uttered will be accountable. And the things done will have the reward suit to it.

The world we live in has the laws that govern nature. And if you do away these laws, then you will cause harm to yourself which cannot heal. Many people have done wrong to their lives and others.

Then again they have caused the accident to others without notice. Some disregard right doing but excuse themselves.

Do not deliberately trap others and later say sorry. Prepare yourself for good and be ready to solve others problem.

Live without hurting others. Be thankful to God and others; serve your little brothers or sisters and the elderly. Promote peace; be kind and love others as yourself.

Share with others about good things and wish them well. Do not be angry without meaning, but prepare yourself to face every wrong thing with a heart.

Do not joke in life but be serious and do your work as a faithful servant. Know how to relate with others and serve them with a heart.

Be a blessing to others and reveal your good thought to them. It will go well with you but be careful in life and know how to manage every situation.

2. Why are you so angry?

There are many bad things we intentionally plan and do. But pretend as if we are not into that idea or act.

There are things done against others but difficult to say sorry. Do not be angry without reason but try to do well and to prevent anger.

The planned sin goes with angry or support anger. Every good work we have done go with joy and encouragement.

But work wrongly done set anger or goes with anger. The good brain goes with good thought and bad goes as the same. If you think well, you behave well. Bad thought comes with bad acts and good thought occurs in good acts.

Food brings good joy, but the hungry stomach goes with anger. And the food prepared for the cat makes the dog angry.

Covetousness goes with anger and the anger destroys good thought and feeling. Do not be lazy, do your work well and do not envy others' property.

Be serious about your work and do not set your mind on others belongings. Work hard and promote yourself by making the right purpose.

Try different avenues and prevent procrastination. Do your best to prevent laziness; keep your time for the best result. Work sufficiently, do not mark time or measure with the time.

Do not abuse yourself with insufficient labour or overwork. But manage your time and bring out a good result. Be diligent in all matters of life and bring out new ideas.

Do not trust or put your confidence in any man but do your business as a faithful servant.

Keep your mindset on the things belongs to you. Control yourself and keep your mind from the things that do not profit.

Shut your mouth from other people's interest. Be pleased with what you have and cherish it.

Go with others but make a difference in your good conduct. Set straight track, do not accept curve or a short way to make money.

Let your words be sufficient, stop bragging and keep silent. Do not be too known but learn new things to better your grade.

Learn to fit every position and do well in your conversation. Do not let others do for you, whiles you can do the best than them.

Always push forward do not look back or turn around by circumstances. Do well and let others know your ability.

Do not be ashamed with the little you have but prove it to others that it is sufficient for your journey.

Do your part as you can and be faithful in the little and the big. The life of this world comprises actions and activities. If you do not do well, you will be late in life and fail.

Do not be angry without reason and never be angry because of your lack. But be honest with your work and whatever you are doing.

If you do well, you will not be angry; but if you did not do well, then you will be angry.

Why are you furious? Or why are you angry? You can prevent envious by making yours decent.

Don't be lazy, do things well and then enjoy a good life. Be alert and forceful; do not go before others or after others but go with them.

Do not rush but make yours unique and be considerate. Why are you angry?

Note: Genesis 4:1-7

Now Adam knew Eve his wife, and she conceived and bore Cain, saying, "I have gotten a man with the help of the Lord." And again, she bore his brother Abel.

Now Abel was a keeper of sheep, and Cain a worker of the ground.

In the course of time, Cain brought to the Lord an offering of the fruit of the ground, and Abel also brought of the firstborn of his flock and of their fat portions.

And the Lord had regard for Abel and his offering, but for Cain and his offering, he had no regard. So Cain was very angry, and his face fell.

The Lord said to Cain, "Why are you angry, and why has your face fallen? If you do well, will you not be accepted? And

if you do not do well, sin is crouching at the door. Its desire is contrary to you, but you must rule over it."

In fact, those who love move with love, and those who hate move with hate.

But those who want to do right, always wish others good, but those who love to do evil, always find fault with others.

Cain became angry with his brother because his works are evil but his brother good. In this world, everyone has what makes his or her life dear.

But everyone has only two options to live his or her life. Everyone have to choose one which is his or her wish to live as a human being.

These options have the end results and the reward it must receive. Have you decided what will make your life dear? What will be the results of it? Why are you angry?

If you do well, will you not be accepted? My brother, everyone will face the realities of life and its result and reward.

What will be your lot? Do you want to live as Cain? You need to consider the way you wish your life. Do what is right and gain the right.

3. Think and Act

Do not close your eyes and do things as the mad man in life. The rivers have their channels and all other things have a lane for a living.

Do not go to the right or to the left without the correct reason. Never fight or talk with no reason. But know the time and hour that is reasonable. And do things that favour's all those around you.

Do not go beyond the line or do not cross the demarcation line. Know the difference between day and the night.

Do not worry when somebody hurt you. Be patient in your speech and know how to communicate with others.

Do not rush when doing something. Consider your speech at each hour and know the time to voice out. Eat sufficiently, do not over eat but measure what is before you, and then prevent greedily.

Do not mislead others with your false thought. Do not frame words that do not benefit. Cause no alarm without a thief; means never draw people's attention for no reason.

Manage your house, not the others and do not conclude your message without meaning.

Always know the right time and the reasonable hour to say no or yes. Make your speech simple and reasonable. Dress decent and wear decent shoes. Means do not be a stumbling block to others.

Do not say any word or add any word concerning what you have been sent to say.

Do not hesitate to do well to others, or give to others what you have. Do not rush to answer a word; if you have been asked to explain something.

Let your no be no, and you're yes be yes. It is your duty to make the choice on two different things.

Never let others decide for you or choose for you as a child. Manage to control yourself when someone causes you to anger.

Do not mutter with one of your workers before his or her colleagues; you need to consider the sun and the moon and the stars.

Means do not separate the best friend by your false conversation. Do not show love to one of your workers than the others. Try to prevent hatred among your employees.

We will be judged by our act or doings. Do not exchange somebody's rights through a bribe, and never turn judgment because of money.

Consider your walk; your speech and so on. Do not pretend to cause harm to your brother or sister. It is better to lose your gold than to let someone fall by your conduct.

Ask when you do not know and seek if it is needed, and nock when you come before at the door of someone's room.

Do not act as if you did not have a mind. Search and study the difference between gold and silver.

Do not mix oil with water to prove your ability; else you will fail because of the differences.

Means never force yourself to do things you don't have any knowledge concerning it; and then to disgrace yourself.

Give the wholesome food to others. Means say the right words to others and let them recognize you.

Do not dance without a song or act like a mad man. For you do not know who is coming, or what will happen in the next hour.

Seek knowledge and wisdom that will help to differentiate the right from wrong.

Do not build the lights around you, whiles you know you are in darkness. Means do not show off and let others admire you through deception.

But be simple and act decency, so that, you will get help when you need help. Do not be wise at your own estimation but be humble and be merciful, then receive mercy.

Do not work with any heart, else you will earn a bad result. We are in the world with confusion and the dangers, but we need to manage all the conditions with a good heart and with reasonable conduct.

When your enemy falls, do not dance at his or her presence. But show sympathy and then prevent provocation.

Do not consider the mocking bird to flee without punishment. That is, punish your child on the wrong act and discipline him or her to take the good path.

Do not support the wrong act but reproof and correct the wrong child. Let your child praise you at your old age.

Do not seek the result of a conversation which you are not part. Why are you stressing yourself on somebody's interest? Think of yourself and consider the result of your life.

Do not be above simplicity in life or how you should live, but consider the life and pick the sufficient which makes life better and desirable.

Do not sound your friend secret to others, but consider the outcome and prevent yourself from damage. Always assumed the result of your act and behave well.

Do not compare an animal with a man on bases of looking down at him. Means do not discourage your brother or sister concerning his or her deficiency. But think and act decently.

4. Don't Rush

Life is not a race and it is not like the sea that is always busy. But it needs patience and control.

The mountain has trees but how can we find out the depth of the soil on top. So is life, we cannot find out the result.

But we can determine the outcome through the act of today's movement. Why are you rushing? Why are you compare or thinking you are late? A tree is not climbed by running; so as to life.

You cannot rush or run to make things done at a moment. As a song is arranged before singing, so life needs arrangement before it can be managed well.

Do not think you are late and you need to do things fast to get a better life.

Days and years are set before us by God and life must track the same. You cannot do anything about it.

As the world consists of darkness and light, so as life be. And you cannot wake up one day and have all your needs on the same day.

As the world wasn't created in one day; so as life needs to be built with that series. The life needs to go by order and it must be built through days and years.

Be patient in whatever you are doing and take heart. Do not rush in speaking. Do not rush in eating; do not rush to answer a question and so on.

In fact, you cannot wash your hands with only soap without water. And again, you cannot go with a single leg and you cannot run with a single led.

It is impossible. You need to understand the series in life and how to cope with all situations.

What do I mean? Everyone needs wholesome characters for his or her life to earn profitable ends.

If you rush, you will miss the needed amenities and cause an accident to your life. Means you will either die before your time or lost a meaningful life.

Do not jump or run in life and again do not mark the time. But consider the way and the manner you behave.

You need to move like a clock move, but don't go before or after the clock. Means keep your time and make use of it.

As you cannot run on the muddy ground, so you cannot run in life. It is better to be late in life than to rush and fail in life.

As it is not lawful to use your two hands to eat; therefore, it is not lawful to rush or run in life.

Do not be too aggressive about your life to make things well. That is, do not force yourself to become rich. But take time, and reason about the best way you can manage to the best of your wish. Why die before your time? Do not rush, for you don't know what tomorrow holds for you. Be patient and keep on managing, then fulfill your goal and earn a good destiny.

5. Don't be Careless

You need to mind your business and value every little thing. Do not take things for granted.

Be serious in life and determine a positive result. Pick the little that have less attention and prepare it with days. Open your eyes and search for the best.

Do not mind to dig deep but consider every stage. Set the target but do not put aside the necessary tools for the life through rushing. Set your goal right but manage the rest.

Do not combine sugar and honey at the same time, but use them one after the other. Prepare yourself at each time and welcome negative and positive. Know the difference between day and night.

Do not misuse the time but make a profit each second. Control yourself at every hour and manage. Do things right but consider the outcome.

Do not move without considering your steps or do not move without your eyes.

Means take care and move. Arrange your kitchen and prepare your food. That is, be decent in all stages of life.

Do not use two knives at the same time. That is, do things one after the other. Do not combine dogs and cats in the same Apartment. That is, you cannot rear two different animals in one cage.

Do not play two songs at the same time. Means do not put yourself into trouble without preparation. Plan and do things in order.

Set the target but manage the target. That is, work towards your goal but do not put aside what benefit others and you.

Do not cut the guideline. Means do not overlook the laws and regulations. Do not talk when you are walking alone.

That is, don't behave like a mad man. Cover your mouth when coughing. Means close your mouth when you are eating.

Do not combine salt and sugar at the same time. That is, do not combine lies with the truth.

Do not leave a stranger alone in your room. That is, do not trust the person you did not know well. Do not answer a word without understanding.

Do not combine oil and water as one substance. Do not use oil to wash your hand like water.

That is, do not replace bad for good or do not do things contrary to the law and order.

Do not sit on somebody's chair without his or her consent. Means do not steal someone's property without his or her approval.

Do not mix two different oils for profit. Means do not cheat others for prosperities sake.

Do not forsake your old house in which you grow. Means do not disrespect your Mother or Father at their old age.

Do not compare two different ropes as the same. Means do not compare two different powers as the same. Go forward do not look back. That is, don't give up or be discouraged.

You need to dress up but do not forget your shoe. That is, don't overdress but dress decently.

Do not let your shoes make a noise when walking on the street. Means dress with no attention towards you or dress modestly with no comments.

Do not talk over time or more than the required hour. Means talk like a reasonable man but not as a fool.

Do not cross a small river on foot when it is raining. Means do not consider a small thing as of no value when you haven't experienced before.

Do not value yourself than others because of your beauty or exalt yourself concerning what you have, for you do not know the difference between today and tomorrow.

Means you do not know what will happen today or tomorrow, so don't laugh at your friend.

Consider the poor and regard the aged at your harvest time. Means give to others who need your help today, for you don't know what tomorrow holds.

It is unnecessary to run in your bedroom or the living room. That is, it is not a good or wise thing to rush when you are eating.

Consider the wind and create windows at your room to keep it from heat. Means welcome people whom you did not know and they will bless you.

Respect the platform on which you are standing and do not run on it but consider its height, and then it will keep you from falling.

Means respect those under you but do not disregard them; for they will let you prosper, and without them: you cannot stand.

Do not go before your master, but follow your master and learn from him. Always ask, if you don't know and don't be too known to cause your life into ruin.

Always try to do the best thing but do not exalt yourself about the good work done. Try to do the best of your time, when you are on duty at your workplace.

Do away laziness and be forceful. Consider every little thing, do not take it as light, else you will lose your dignity. Plan and do things in order.

Never start your work without prayer. Be practical and manage any condition.

Do not be too high or do not be too simple, but be modest in the manner of no comments.

Manage to welcome everyone and speak well or be attentive to anyone who you communicate with.

Be ready always and set your goals well, do not discourage by circumstance but go forward.

Do not conclude your word without your viewers understanding, but make it clear to promote their peace.

Do not leave without concluding of your case, but settle it as it stands on you for peace. Know how to walk and talk in the house of God.

Let your prayers be simple and reasonable.Do not pray to please men, but pray from the heart and in humility.

Stop conversation at the courtroom and consider your speech before the judge.

Respect and shut your mouth in the presence of the king. Do not be haste to answer a question but be considerate when answering.

Do not push yourself into trouble when there is no trouble. Means keep yourself at all times from the words of others.

Do not go before the thief or robber, else you will be adding by his or her punishment. Consider every act you proceed, and then have the good results. Do not say yes when the word is not true.

Do not shout when you are speaking to anybody. But consider your speech carefully in front of the rulers.

Do not cry at the wedding premises even when you do not agree. But control yourself till the end. That is, be wise and do the right thing in the presence of the mass congregation.

Do not joke before a lion, whiles you don't have a leg to run. That is, do not annoy the king in his palace with a false act without redeemer or the advocate.

Do not put your leg on somebody's shoulder and laugh at the same time. Means do not cheat your brother and convince him with your false words of comfort.

Do not mix salt and sugar in your mouth. That is, makes your words or speech clear for everyone to hear you well. Or do not deceive others by your words.

6. Understanding the Life

God created the world in days and through this process makes the life whole.

In fact, the world has a lot of histories and messages that need attention. As human beings, we need to consider everything that goes on every day.

Humans' lives have a lot of lessons and the subjects that need to be studied. Things that happen every day are calling us out to be watchful. We have so many incidents which serve as security.

Life cannot be straight or smooth every day. What we need to know is to manage and consider every situation. Things of this world have no peace and proper standing.

Many people have failed because of impatient and have damaged their life because of the lack of waiting.

We must understand life and how it must be controlled. In this world, nothing comes by accident, but it is for our lessons and promotions or failures.

Life is subjected to failures and dangers, but all these are there for our progress.

We must keep in mind that, we cannot enjoy good continuously, but sudden risk and others are part of our progress.

We should not make a noise when something bad happens to us. But we should know is part of life.

There are many sounds of cry every day, and there is a joy as well. This life is mixed with good and bad because of our first parent sin.

The world has been damaged by sin. So things are not accurate as it was from the beginning.

This has made life too hard for us as human beings. We have the keys which can open every good thing that makes life better.

But there is attack everywhere on the globe, which always resists us from reaching the best standard. And because of these attacks, you need to determine and have faith in God.

It is tough to manage life; if you are not determined. You can give up and do whatever you wish but later destroy your life forever.

Too much poverty can destroy your ability and can even shut you till the grave.

Try and do something that will set your life at liberty and peace; and then continuing in searching for the best that makes others get benefit from you.

Do not fill up your cap only but fill others cap too. Means do not be selfish but support others of their needs.

You must understand that this world is not for the one man but for everyone born in it. That is, try to share with others what you have and enjoy with them and weep with them.

Do not cover your belonging for your own benefits; but let others use as their own property, that makes your blessings complete and enjoyable.

You cannot complete your life without support from others. So, let others complete theirs with your support.

Do not be hard, but be flexible but not weak. Be humble but not dangerous. Be smart but not as the thief. Do not deceive by your appearance but do what people will admire you.

Try to live peacefully with your enemies but don't hate them; do them good and let them know you love them. It is difficult to love your enemy but that makes you unique.

Try and understand all these conditions, and then you will be fruitful. A good life is not like a running river which everyone can fetch and drink.

But it is like facing the desert wind blowing with dust. But requires forcefulness; perseverance, willingness and focused in order to pass through.

Those without these characters; will fail of a good life and its practice. Do not consider the sea wind or look to the waves but be focus and drive your boat to the shore.

So many people have failed because of cheap life and unfaithfulness. Those who want cheap life disregard the principles of a good life and how it must live.

The good life has penalties and that penalties are the beacons of correct progress in life. You need to know the circumstances in life and how it must be managed.

Those who take note and keep in mind with correct heart makes the difference. But those who disregard and take the life as anything, abuse themselves.

Do your best and record the songs of life to better your life. Means take notes of every situation and set your life with the correct goal, and then harvest the peak of life.

Life stands on the way you want it. Everyone must know the reality of life and how we should live.

As you cannot do away the footing of a building, so you cannot start life in the middle stage.

You need to start the life from scratch and end in the matured stage. That is, you must succeed in life whatever may be.

Do not fill with sorrow when things become tough. But consider as a helping tool for your progress.

Master yourself through hardships and discover the best for your life. Do not be dismay or fear, but prove yourself as a workman who knows the best for the client.

Means makes your work as experience man whether you have experienced or not. So far as it is your fields do it excellently.

God will not try you according to what you cannot do, but on what you can do. Always try your best and do what you can, but don't be abused by the trial. You need to understand life in all matters of conditions but be serious at every stage.

Do not cry when you hurt by someone, it is part of life. Do not be annoyed by trials or angry on the basis of hardship you are going through. But be prudent and make it profitable.

7. Manage to Prevent Sorry

We always wrong in life every day but some pretend or intentionally wrong their friends and others.

Some also consider wrong as nothing. But you cannot joke before a lion and take yourself free.

Do not consider an ant as of no value or feeble to do and then promote the elephant as the king of capable.

Means do not look down on others who are less in stature and then admire the giant bodies. Do not consider giant bodies as those who can do as to the best.

Do not leave your master without seeking permission and later say I am sorry. Do not approach the king in his chamber without knocking. Consider the base of a building before starting the structure.

Do not wrong your master and leave him and later beg him for pardon. Be at peace with your master always and work from the heart.

Be respectful and diligent in labour. Do not abuse your work mate with false accusations and later seek peace with him or her.

Consider every step you make and try to prevent regretful. Do your best to promote peace with all men and manage every condition.

Do not leave the palace with running but consider your steps before the king.

Control your speech with time and prevent errors from your speech. Means know how to speak each time to others and then prevent sorry after the speech. Keep your time and prevent lateness at your workplace.

Do to others as you wish them to do for you. Be thankful and prevent greediness.

Share equally to others who you work with when gifts are given to be shared with them. Put outside envy in work when you are working with your colleagues.

Do your best to encourage your associates in labour. Do not work to please men but be faithful in your work and harvest the best result. Again never cheat in labour and later reveal your false labour.

Do not frame false news to distort the air but consider your speech and let the air blow at ease.

Means do not confuse people by misleading them by your false message. Always find out the truth and promote peace.

Do not force yourself to be somebody by your appearance or do not carry the title you have no idea. Never wear the shoe that is more than your size and to cause yourself trouble.

Mind your word and polish it from mistakes. When you borrow, fulfill the payment; do not close your eyes on it.

Be faithful in your speech and do not lie for favour. Set your apartment with good atmosphere and then welcome people with good attention.

Means do not confuse people for your own curse by misleading them and to hurt yourself at the end.

Always set your head up and consider the little. That is, mind those around you and consider the child as well. Study to the best end and then do your research well, to prevent distrust.

Do not run on the rough road with all your strength, but manage with the walk to prevent hurt.

That is, keep your eyes with all matters of situation to prevent damage to yourself and others.

Set your goal with the correct level to prevent stress. That is, do not attempt what is not your field to disgrace yourself.

Always wash your hands in running water to prevent sickness. Means do the right things and then get good results.

Speak with a salt to prevent tasteless from your speech. Means avoid useless talk in your speech.

Do not throw stones at night to disturb your community without meaning. That is, do not make noise on reasonable hours at the night with sound sleep. Do not bath with your shoes at home. Means do not act as a thoughtless.

Always do things in the light to prevent damage. Means let others witness about your doings with good comments.

Do not work with measuring the time or keep your mind on time. But avoid measuring the time and work tirelessly but do not abuse yourself with overwork.

Do not consider the work as of whether small or big but do what you can by the truth, and from the correct heart.

Do not trust a man by his word but by his act. Never turn around and say it is done, whiles you know nothing has been done.

Means do not lie to others on the bases of protecting yourself. Do not forget your keys when leaving home. Means prepare your-self well at any time.

Welcome two people equally, do not show partiality by regarding the one than the other.

Do the right thing. Do not deceive by your appearance or pretend as gold. Avoid show without acts or comments.

That is, do not appear as a wealthy man or woman without capital. Do not jump before your enemy but consider your step at his or her presence. That is, seek peace and always do right at the presence of your enemy.

Do not accept the case with only one witness but consider two witnesses for the judgment.

Do not put aside the right judgment or twist the judgment on the bases of enticement.

Consider every case well and conclude with the right judgment. Do not put aside the witnesses of any case brought to you as a judge.

Then and again consider every little word before the pronouncement of the judgment.

Everyone has only a chance about his or her life to live. So do not kill someone by your word or act about anything you undertake.

Do not throw out or disregard the leftover grains, for it is food for the birds of the air.

That is, do not be selfish and keep all the food for yourself. But share or give out to others who need your help.

Do not put off the light of the house to cause somebody's fall or hurt. But put on the light to keep the house from the darkness. That is, keep on entertaining others on your good works or acts.

But do not prevent others by your bad acts or behaviour. Do not lie to your husband or wife on the basis of your selfish interest. But consider and tell the truth and promoting continuous peace and love.

Do not go before or after your husband or wife, when you are going to the same place. But move with or go together to strengthen the continuous faithfulness and to prevent disunity.

That is, keep closer to yourselves for profound love. Prevent conversation without introducing the friend or mate to the husband or wife as you are going together.

Dress together and move together; that is, do not cover up anything to the wife or the husband.

Pour out the honey from its cup and share together the sweets and rejoice together.

Appreciate the doings and prevent discouragement. Continue the dance to the end of the song to keep happiness to the end.

Do not over dance to abuse the sweetness of the song, but keep it on the track to prevent an accident. Manage to prevent sorry and consider the move.

Do not praise one child among your children or before the other children. Always keep silence or stop your conversation when you heard the noise at your backyard. That is, do not continue your speech, when there is a misunderstanding between you and your spouse.

Be silent when there is a shout or misunderstanding, to keep your continuous peace.

Manage the bottom and the top. That is, cope with all the conditions or the situations with the good heart and patience.

Do not go beyond miles but the end with your mile and then prevent disrespect. That is, obey the rules of nature.

Do not overflow in your speech as a madman but control your speech and make your words simple and understandable. Always tell the truth and prevent confusion. Based on the facts and defend your case.

Put off the clumpy act and respect the aged. Be happy and manage the little or the big. Be thankful to God and move with all your good works and acts.

8. Do the Right Thing

Do not close your eyes and walk, but open your eyes and see. Do the right thing.

Do the right thing, do not say yes, whiles the answer is no. do not run before your parents but run after them.

Do the right thing. Many people want to fill up their rooms and leave the whole building. Means do not hoard up by selfishness but give to others as you can.

Do the right thing. Respect men and wish them well. Do the right thing. Dress well, when leaving from home.

Arrange your bed before leaving. That is, do not close your eyes from your responsibilities. Do the right thing. Do not sweep your room and leave your corridor unprepared. That is, complete your responsibilities each day.

Do not put the light under the table, but on the table. Means do not cover what benefit others but share with them.

Do the right thing whiles you have life. Help the needy and rescue the perishing. Share the big and small at the hours of want. Go with charity and truth always, and then seek to help the weak.

Do the right thing! Do not look down on others because of your wealth. Do not eat to the bottom but leave the rest to the birds. That is, do not be selfish concerning what you have, but give to others who need your help.

Do not leave the old woman or man alone to struggle. Means do not close your eyes from the destitute or the weaker that need your donation. Do the right thing!

Do not take away the sightless stick to cause him or her fall. That is, do not cheat the stranger at your home about his or her needs.

Do the right thing! Do not pass through the window, whiles there is a door. Means do things according to the required measures.

Do not sleep on the bed contrary to yours. Means do not take somebody's wife like yours.

Do not go and shout at the front of kings' palace out of consideration. That is, do not go beyond the demarcation or break the moral law.

Always seek to prevent war in the presence of your enemy and love at all times. Do the right thing! Keep on your donations and do not consider your giving by means of seeking the reward.

Help the stranger but consider your room, that is, serve the stranger as well but be vigilant.

Do not leave your keys for the one you do not know. Keep your eye on the ground and consider every weed.

That is, know how to deal with others for good but with the eyes open. Rejoice with those who are in good condition and at the same time mourn with those who are mourning.

Do not leave the food uncovered and do not give to the stranger the unwholesome food. Do not mislead the stranger by cheating. But honour the stranger with a good welcome.

Do not go before the stranger or after the stranger who did not know where to step his or her feet. Do the right thing! Set the time well to prevent lateness.

Do not delay the worker's payment to keep on their worries. But pay prompt their wages and to prevent curse.

Do not argue with your worker on his payment. Do not force your worker to work overtime but consider his strength and health.

Do not put your worker into trouble because of your wealth. Give a reasonable amount of payment to your worker to prevent murmuring against you.

Do not let your worker cry before to receiving his or her payment. Give and continue in giving, support and makes people laugh with a good heart.

Do not close your door and shout people's out from your presence. Means welcome people with a good heart and with love. Complete your work with the correct report and the best result.

Do not use your tools for making unnecessary things. But let your tools work excellently.

9. Burning the weeds

Do not support the growth of weeds in your field. Do your best to throw out the poisonous substance or burn out the weeds in your field.

Do not support the wicked on his or her actions. Throw out the crack bottle and fill the fresh one.

That is, do not waste your time on the unnecessary things. But make use of the time on the things that benefit.

Every fresh thing needs fresh and every old thing needs old. As you cannot dress a child with the aged attire, so to the life we are living. You cannot take life contrary to its principles.

Whatever you are doing must be on its way. What do I mean or want to say concerning this content; burning the growing weeds?

Every practice in this world forms the character and grows for harvest.

The life we are living needs carefulness every day and night. We need not rest or stop in the way for the needless things.

We need not entertain any weeds to occupy our fields of productions. That is, do not allow anything to entice you from your improvement.

That is, determine on the things that bring peace to the soul. Do away covetousness; selfishness, fornication, greedy, malice and so on. These are the weeds that make life standstill and then destroy the idea of life and make things worse.

You need to know the best for your life and the fruit you must bear.

Do not cover the bucket when it is raining. Be ready at all time and make use of every minute.

Do not allow someone to use your cup for drinking. That is, do not allow people to look down on you because of your act or do not devalue yourself because of your poverty.

This world has so many influences and the things that can destroy the soul for eternity.

Every act forms character and decides the position of the actor or the actress.

Do not joke or jump before the lion as your playmate. Do not consider the drop of water as small or disregard the little act or doings as nothing.

Who knows the penalties of one sin committed? Do not take things for granted, every little substance has the value and its performance.

Do not allow or entertain the stranger food on your table. Do not look the wine or considers its smoothness, it bites like a scorpion.

Do not take note of a woman or thought of her beauty, it destroys the spiritual giant. In fact, all the things on this world or everything which is done on this earth has the effect or the affect at the end.

But the one who considers and manage according to the right channel find his or her-self secure.

We shouldn't allow the matters of this world take us captive. We need to shun everything that entices us into trouble.

Do not love the world or the things in the world; the one who loves the world has no love for God.

This world is passing away but one who considers God will live. So, do not allow weeds to take over your farm or field.

But clear the field with all the needed tools and then find rest and peace for your soul. The world is going to an end but what will be your lot?

How have you considered your act and doings? Every plant that does not produce good fruit will be root out. Do not nurse the fruitless plant on your field or allow the growth of weeds. But do your best to care for the field, and everything on it.

And then burn the unwanted materials from it. What do I want you to know? Do not joke or allow things to take you captive.

Take your life seriously and do things right and then fulfill your mission on this earth.

Do not dismantle your treasure or destroy your gold. But make things well and protect your soul from eternal doom.

Do not fill the broken bottles but fill the fresh bottles and then avoid waste. That is, do not waste your time on the needless things but on the necessary ones. Do not wash the pig in the early morning but wash it at the night and protect your cloth.

Consider your doing and prevent yourself from damage.Do not water the unplanted field for the sake of preventing dust.

That is, do not give to one who needs nothing or avoids giving to the rich and then prevents the curse to the entire family.

But refresh others by giving to the poor and then refresh yourself. Burn the growing weeds and then secures your place.

Continuing on your good works but consider and avoid doing the things that are unprofitable.

Do not entertain evil at your doorstep to allow it into your room. Be vigilant and do things according to its right channel.

Burn the growing weeds from your field. That is, keep your heart than anything that needs to be preserved.

10. When shall I be call?

What I mine going to answer, when the master calls me? Who will be my lawyer and how is my case will be ending me?

In fact, we have case with the Master and matters that need to be solve. Our history as human beings has a big mark which no balm can heal.

There is a death sentence upon us all as human beings. There is no signal that is prompting us on this matter. No one knows when the death will claim each of us. It always happen unexpected or take us captive unaware.

Our life is at risk each moment with no signals. Oh what a tragedy life! A life, that consists of penalties and death which take us captive without notice. This is serious life that each one needs to be care about it.

There is no second chance or any time again for transformation. When you lose it, you lose forever. Life is precious than gold and silver.

It is peak of all matters that owns everything. There is nothing to compare with life; it is above everything and precious than everything calls precious.

Life is short in humans lives due to sin committed by our first parents. We are all at risk and there is no favor at all.

When it turn to you; gone forever. When shall you be called? What will you do? Is there any answer you can give? Oh my dear! We have serious case with the master.

It is appointed for us to die once and after there is judgment which no one can escape.

When He calls you, what will you answer? When shall I be call? I do not know, and if I would be call, what will be my reward?

Each one of us needs to think and then behave well; for we have case with the Master. Have you consider yourself well? What do you find? What do you do about it? Is it good or wrong? Will it be well with you, when you are called?

You need to consider your life and then rethink about your deeds. You have case with the Master.

This life is meaningless and there is no profit about it. I mean it does not last as it should be. It is different from what you think for, and different from how you imagine.

It is not fair as you want it to be, and it cannot be as you need it. It varies and cannot be equal. You can imagine but you cannot have it as you wish it.

Oh what a world we live! Sin has damage and crooks everything. Everyone is suffering, whether faithful or not, righteous or not. What shall we do and what can we do? Oh! This battle is tough and difficult to interpret.

In all, what will be your reward? Do you know when you will be call? We do not know when death will claim each one of us. What we do know is to prepare every day. Do you know when your mouth will close?

Do you know when your hands will be bending at your back? We have penalty before us which needs preparation to face it.

Our life is like vapor, which disappears without returns. We cannot know how it will come, but we can prepare when it comes. Our only hope is to take Christ as our personal savior. He is the way; the truth and the life.

Know that, you cannot escape death but you can have life after when believe Jesus Christ dearly. When shall you be call or die?

No one knows, yet prepare and be ready for it. It is appointed for us all. What will be your reward after?

11. What will happen after?

Every tree that is planted bears fruit. So, is the every deed proceeding? Everyone is going to receive his or her reward through the performance revealed. We have rewards with the Master which is equal to the deeds.

What are you going to receive when the Master comes? It is not all when you die, but there is a judgment. Everyone is going to receive his or her price when turns to him or her according to the work done.

Whatever you do, you will be harvested. Great men are not always wise, nor do the aged always understand justice. Do not consider yourself as the mighty, yet be humble and know the time.

But there is a spirit in a man, and the breath of the Almighty that gives him understanding.

Whatever the case, everyone is going to face the fruit of his or her deeds. Someone will say or ask, if you die, is it all? Or is there anything again after death?

What do I mean about this content? What will happen after? The Bible has made it clear that there is a judgment after death. If there is judgment, then there will be resurrection.

This death that we see is a first death, and also it is a sleep. The time is coming when everyone will be rise from the death.

Those who believe God and accept Jesus Christ as their personal savior will be resurrected when He comes in the second time. Those who did not accept Him would be dead with those who are already dead for thousand years.

When the thousand years are over, Christ will come on this earth again with the saints who had life at His second return with the Holy City (The New Jerusalem) to this earth.

Those who did not receive their share at His second return will have their reward after the thousand years.

Here, the fire will come down from Heaven and then consume them. This will be the reward of those who did not have chance to enter Heaven within the second coming of Christ. Here, Christ will pay the wicked according to their deeds by fire and brimstone.

There is a reward for every deeds or work. So, this life is not all, yet there will be reward. What have you considered? Do you respect? What are your deeds? The world will receive it due by it deeds.

Do not deceive yourself and never make yourself light whiles you are dark. Do not pretend to be good, whiles you know it is not so. Stop pretending and then do things right and according.

We all have case with the Master. If you look around what do you see? What is going on? What are you doing? What is your share? How do you do your things? This is not all, yet there will be a reward for each deed.

Many people think that there would be no judgment after this life. Others also think that this life is all, there is nothing again. Do not joke of this life and never waste your time on things that are not necessary.

You need to consider yourself well and then do things right. This life is not all, yet there is another thing after this.

Do not be wise at your own estimation to destroy yourself. But consider the outcome and then behave well.

This life is not all, yet there is judgment which nothing can be compared. My dear, we have case with the Master, so know how to behave and then do things according to the requirements. There is judgment and reward after this life.

12. Will this be good results?

You shall receive the reward according or equal to work done. Every farmer harvest fruit of the tree he or she planted. So, your deeds will determine your results. It depends on your deeds or your acts that you always do.

This life has lot to face and a lot to demand. Whatever we exhibit determines the outcome and then makes the reward. Your achievement resulted by your work done. So, also your reward confirms your achievement.

What results do you want to achieve? How did you live? What have you considered? How did you go about? Our actions determine the life we will live and then set the goals ahead of us. What have you done?

What do you want to achieve? There are many things ahead of us but what will these things will lead us to? Have you consider those things and how have you determine to go with? Is there anything that entices you?

What is your interest? How did you live your life? Oh! Who will save me from all these troubles? This life is hard for me and I cannot go without (You) oh God! Will this be your word?

If you accept your condition, and then consider God, your life will be worthy. Do not let the world lead you.

Never accept to live a cheap life, yet value your being and then live faithful. Do not go with smart people, but go with God fearful men and obtain wisdom.

Do not take the world and then leave God, yet consider God first and then live your life. Why die before your time? Though things are fighting against you both spiritual and physical, yet hold your dignity to the end.

Do not throw yourself down because of poverty. Never abuse yourself due to force of the earth.

Always know that, there is a reward for every deed. You need to consider every little thing and then value it. For you do not know what your dream will end.

Fight the good fight of faith and then hold the truth to end. Do not force yourself to do things that are contrary to the laws of nature. But consider the outcome and then keep yourself well. If you keep this in mind, then you will be safe.

The world has teachers that teach every day lessons of life, but what will those lessons will lead you to? This comes in the content, will this be good results?

If it will be, it depends on the acts been exhibited. Do not take things for granted, and never go where you are not allowed to go. Know how to walk; know how to talk, know how to dress and prevent short comings.

For all these things will be bringing into judgment. So, it is your turn to proof yourself as a faithful man.

Do you have a lawyer? Will your lawyer will be able to save you? If it is so, then it depends on your ability that you proof in life.

Do not disturb yourself about the world goods, neither wish things as without law. But live a life without a question mark. As it stands on you, do your best to glorify God. Be faithful like Job; stand boldly as Daniel, and then live like Noah.

These people are faithful and God is pride about their life and their integrity. Will this be good results? Yes, if we stay in as we have been taught.

This life is not all, yet there is a judgment after. But the time is not known by anyone.

I wish you well, but be considerate in all things. Will this be good results? It will be determine by your doings and faith in Christ.

13. Who knows the evil hour?

As the sleep come without notification, so evil hour comes without sound of awareness.

It comes as a thief in the night with no notice. A life cannot be certain without hope and there is nothing that grow without nursing.

The world has so many things but good life depend on principles. Who can tell good or bad times ahead of us?

Whatever the life will be; there is hope, unless we disregard it. Do not show yourself as you know everything, yet be considerate and learn other things from humility.

Do not raise your shoulders, because of your power. Do not walk over others for your strength sake. How can tree grow without rain, means without God you are nothing. It seems you are great in your own eyes.

A little child can teach you a lesson. Many leaders sometimes disregard their servants; yet some of them do not know that, without their servants, they are not leaders.

There are stages in life and also lessons that needs to be study at each stage. Without humility, these lessons cannot be known. Means you cannot bear any fruit without humility.

You need to come down, for where you are standing is too high. Do not miss your flight because of your name. Watch out and keep your time for the sake of your future.

When will you come down from where you are standing? You can turn to everywhere you like; but know that, there is a reward for each deed.

Who knows the evil hour? It seems you are giant and strong and you do not fear anything?

You have not seen what you should see? And you haven't heard what you must hear. Yet know that, there is accountability.

Who knows the evil hour? Do not be wise at your own estimation and never abuse yourself through bribe. But fear God and eschew evil.

Who knows the evil day? Do not oppress others who are weak and never step on the servant due to your wealth.

Know that you shall reap whatever you will sow. No one knows the evil day and no one can tell the outcome or the results; so be considerate and set yourself apart. Whatever the life has the profit, whether good or bad.

Everyone will face the realities of life matters, it does not matter your beauty; wealth and strength. Know that, there will be an evil day.

Can you escape? Be considerate and then open your eyes well and then watch. Watch out! There is a word coming that no one can explain it.

Know that you can meet a case without your knowledge. Be careful and then watch your steps; your mouth and your actions well.

Do not disturb yourself in the world, yet know how you will live in. do not pick things on your chest yet pick them one after another.

But know the best and pick that one. Who knows the evil hour? Do not leave your home without preparation, yet put things together and leave.

Means try and do things right through plan and preparation to fulfill your purpose in life.

Be ready always and set your goal right for the benefit of you and others. Do not throw your dignity aside but make sure you are on the line.

Prepare yourself and set your time well to prevent late in this evil days. Be considerate always and live upright.

In fact, many people joke of life and regardless of its penalties. Others do not mind what will come; in fact they do not know how serious the results will be.

Everyone must learn how to be ready for any life regardless the season. That is, we must be ready to respond any call that will come, because we cannot escape death and judgment. Who knows the evil day?

14. The beginning of Pain

In the beginning, God created the heavens and the earth. The earth and everything in them purposely created for man as his eternal home.

All the things created were good and lovely. Then and again God created a garden called Eden, with all kinds of beautiful things. And the food that to sustain life was made for man.

There was nothing lacking or needful that was out which will benefit the man exempted from his life. That is, all necessary things needed were provide to make the man whole were not out.

The man and his wife were perfect in stature and exquisite. They were created in the likeness of God and the image. So, the man was like God in beauty, in stature and in perfect. God did not create this world in chaos but to dwell in peace and comfort.

Everything was in order and pleasant for the man. But God put the test that will keep his perfect being continuously before the man.

Every perfect object needs to be test by a negative; to keep the uniqueness of that object and to prove the beauty of that mechanism for good performance.

You will not agree why perfect thing needs to be test; and why God created the tree of knowledge of good and the evil?

But the negative serve as the security to keep the continuous of goodness in the world. There was nothing good or perfect exempted from trials. So, every trial proofs the maturity of every perfect thing.

The world was not created without negative, but with a negative to apply our choice or the willpower.

Then not accuse God as tyrant. But to maintain fairness and order in the world, there must be a free will for everyone. That is why God does not force us to obey him, but it is our duty.

Many people want to live by sentiment and to do away law and order. I asked myself what transpire and why sorrows every day in globe?

There is one thing we need to know; and to keep in mind that there can be no happiness, if we continue disregard God. Never and ever think that, God wants us to die that is why He put that tree for our test. It is not so. But He (God) needs our love and respect.

Why man was dismisse or thrown from Eden and what is the main reason? As I have already stated that man were the crown being of the universe and the overseer of the all creatures.

Those things under his control must be perfectly care and manage as to the law of God demand. But the man could not sustain his dignity as an administrator.

The reason was that he did not trust God's word as spoken to him and respected not the deity. But listening to unknown voice and done a stupid thing.

In the Garden of Eden, there was a tree of life which can keep man from dying. And in order not to experience another devil as the heaven has experienced before; God dismissed the man from Eden to prevent him from eating the tree of life; to avoid him from staying forever.

So the cherubim were placed, before the tree of life with flame sword to keep the tree of life.

Here the man was throw out to go and till the ground whence he was taken. In this world, every tenant who is stubborn on his land lord would be dismissing from the house he lives.

If you could not sustain your dignity you will be a foolish at the end. Here begins mans' grief and terrible death decree. Today, many wants to live as they wish to avoid the laid down rules or obeying the word of God.

This world has the owner and we need to fear and honour him. Adam sin has brought a lot of tragedies in the world.

The peak of sin is beyond control; but still many people love to commit the same sin which has damage our world.

Why misunderstanding and difficulties among us in this world? Can you imagine the dense of the sadness Adam when he was first sacked from Eden?

How can you describe that hour or the condition of the man? Today's hardship can teach you a bit of the condition of the man at that moment. How do you live your life? Have you considered? Just think of it.

15. The Hardship Conditions

Why jobless; poverty, fruitless and famine? When Adam was sacked from home because of sin, there was no food outside Eden to be eaten.

The man has to work for his food through sweating to get food to eat. That is his first punishment.

Outside Eden, the lands were not like the Eden vegetation; why because curse was pronounced against the rest of the land, and again there was no rain to better the growth of the planted seeds.

Can you imagine the first time the man needs to search for his own food because of sin?

Consequently, the land was not rich even to yield the fruit for him immediately. So, the man needs to work hard for his own food and not like the first.

Your sin today can make a home for you tomorrow; and your stubbornness will determined the kind of hardship you must face.

What do we see today and what can we do about what is going on? Can we be able to do away or ceased to sin? Why famine and poverty?

Why disease and death? Why war and killings? Why misunderstanding? Why childless and so on?

Today's world wasn't like the beginning. Things have changed entirely. God created the world perfectly and orderly.

There is nothing short or to blame whether little; small or big. Then and again there was nothing without purpose whether advantage or disadvantage, they all serve for the man good.

What transpire? In fact, if you look at the condition of man today testifies how sin has brought us to.

The beginning of man was sweet and beautiful. Everything work together for only good and there was no stress in labor or sweat to the extent like today.

But the man was to work for his continuous health and for good exercise to make his being fit to the standard.

The work given to man was to prolong his life and makes him sound for every day duties and the activities. The work was to give man happiness and wealth for multiplication of productions. Then and again work was to make the man improve and to develop as well.

In the Garden of Eden the man need not to till the ground or to plant for food, but to dress and to keep it. Means there was no need to work for food, but to dress and to keep the already made.

Here Adam was to preserve the fruits; herbs and the rest from the weeds, and to keep the environment from over weeds; to clean and to dress.

That is to make place pleasant at all times and above all to make the Garden attractive and order.

Moreover, there wasn't any lack that needs to search for, concerning the possessions and the means. Here everything was obvious for Adam and the work given to him was cheap.

There was no stress in labor or the unproductive in labor; but everything was perfect and enjoyable. The life was beautiful; comfortable, peaceful and pleasant. In fact, Adam was fortunate than any man in the world.

He was handsome and perfect in stature, fit and able man. There wasn't any comparable in creation, he was the image of

God and his likeness, the first man and the manager of all the things created and above all the honorable.

It was Adam who named the creatures both living and nonliving on the earth and the air. There was harmony between the man and the creatures. There was no disturbance between the man and the nature. Everything was in order; good and beautiful.

One thing we all need to ask is who caused our problems today? Sin has been already permitted, but we can do something about it to reduce our hardship, but if we consider God and continue our submissive to Him, we shall succeed.

Today's hardship comprises our thought and acts, though Adam has caused our ruin and the death. But we are part of our problems.

There is no happiness for the sinful; but the one who keep God in mind will be keeping in peace. The peak of Adam sin has covered countless good things that can bring us joy. Every unnoticed word of God can cause us doom forever. But the one who obey the dot; the jot or the least will be called the greatest on the earth and the heaven! The one whose life is the best and reasonable in the sight of God is the one who consider the jot from the word of God.

It is not by many words or the any word, but every word that proceeded out from God mouth will let the man live.

Adam did not consider the dot from the word of God and that caused his death penalty.

Today's hardship results from yesterday disobedient, and there is no war without the source. So the hardship condition results from unnoticed the tiniest word of God. Have you considered? Have you think about?

16. The Birth and Death

Oh! Have you ever consider the life today? What have you thought concerning birth and death? Where from this dying?

In the beginning God created the heavens and the earth; and the earth was formless and empty.

This world was created out from nothing, means it wasn't form from any material thing at anywhere but came as new from the creator's word.

There was a purpose of setting up this earth and the reason of that creation. Mean the world was created by God for a purpose.

The earth was created for man as his eternal home and it is exempted from any chaos, death or any other of disaster. This world was purposely designed for dwelling and beautifully planned for a man to develop it.

In Genesis Chapter 1: 28 says; and God blessed them and said to them, be fruitful and multiply and fill the earth and subdue it.

This indicate that, the man and his family must develop the land and to take care of the things on it forever and ever.

There was no death but birth; there was no pain in birth but peace and joy. There was no sickness but health, and there was no disaster but peace. So, it is not God purpose for a man to die or sick in any way.

But what transpired? In fact, God gave the man mandate to give birth and to be fruitful and multiply. There was no death, or any tragedy been pronounced to the man concerning his life?

The world was perfect and beautiful ordered; peaceful atmosphere and good vegetation's everywhere.

The man was capable in doing and able to control. God created the world permanently, that is eternally to be dwell forever.

In fact, this world purposely gave to a man as his eternal home with no other being. That is, not to share with any other created being. It is his house, home and property.

The man was to rule and manage as well or to have dominion over all the nature; to keep and to dress permanently.

This world was his gift and home eternally. The reason was to dwell as his apartment and kingdom.

But to be a good manage or ruler, his life was subjected to two options to test his faithfulness.

But the man could not pass the test; and then results the death with the birth. Now, the world has change because of sin and the live is subjected to penalties and death.

We are living with the two options; whether eternal life or death, but it depends on sowing; that determine the harvest reward. In fact, there was no death with the birth but there was an option.

There was no pain with the birth but joy. There was no severe sweat in the work, but there was fitness and wealth.

There was no lost but gain, and there was no fruitless but fruitful. There was no waste but useful; and there was no unnecessary but necessary.

Everything was useful and the reason as it was to serve for good. The man and his wife were both naked but were not ashamed.

There was perfect peace and joy. Oh dear, can we have this again? Sure; through submissive to the word of God.

They fit together in movement (the man and his wife) and stay in understanding and truth. There was no short or unfit in their activities and again no lack of anything needed for the life to fit as beings.

They lack nothing in their move. This world was perfect and ordered. But the man (Adam) could not maintain that atmosphere but disregard it.

In the Garden of Eden and it environment was pretty and abundant of fruits; vegetables, crops and herbs which support health and wealth. There was no need of fire to prepare or cook food.

Everything was ready when needed. There was tree of life which can keep the man eternally. The tree of knowledge of good and evil was there to keep the man faithfulness and to sustain his integrity.

There was nothing to causes the man harm if he continues to obey. They were all support his being and work together for his good; whether negative or positive; the animals, the trees and so on.

There was no waste or dead thing among the nature; everything has it purpose and the functioning.

Why death instead of birth only? Why sorrow instead of joy only? Why disaster instead of peace? The world we live today has change because of disobedient and has damage because of sin.

Many people are still continuing in breaking the laws of nature as was the first man.

People do not regard God but regardless through their acts and wishes. Many people intentionally do evil and support it growth; others plan and act wrongly. The age of man has been reduced through peak of sin; and others are dying without hope.

There are alarming of death every day; people are crying day and night. Sorrow increases each day and night, and the disaster sprung up each moment.

There are sounds of fear each day and the earth cannot carry the weight of sin. Many people are going to their eternal homes because of sin and there is no hope of return.

The world is going to an end; the shadows of death have increased. The world has lost the glory and purpose of which it was created. The man was no more as from the beginning; the death has over taken the birth.

The man has lost his nature and his dominion over the earth; because of the regardless of the word of God. Have you considered?

For Knowledge and Good Living
BBS LIFE BOOKS
Don't Miss Your Flight | Page

About the Author

Bernard Benson Sarfo is an acquainted architectural designer and a motivational speaker.He is a gifted teacher who continues to motivate and encourage many.

Read more at https://www.amazon.com//author/bbslifebooks.